America
in the
20th Century

(1913–1999)

by Victor South

LIGHTB◆X
openlightbox.com

LIGHTBOX

Go to
www.openlightbox.com
and enter this book's
unique code.

ACCESS CODE

L B X X 2 8 8 4

Lightbox is an all-inclusive digital solution for the teaching and learning of curriculum topics in an original, groundbreaking way. Lightbox is based on National Curriculum Standards.

STANDARD FEATURES OF LIGHTBOX

 AUDIO High-quality narration using text-to-speech system

 ACTIVITIES Printable PDFs that can be emailed and graded

SLIDESHOWS Pictorial overviews of key concepts

 VIDEOS Embedded high-definition video clips

 WEBLINKS Curated links to external, child-safe resources

TRANSPARENCIES Step-by-step layering of maps, diagrams, charts, and timelines

 INTERACTIVE MAPS Interactive maps and aerial satellite imagery

 QUIZZES Ten multiple choice questions that are automatically graded and emailed for teacher assessment

 KEY WORDS Matching key concepts to their definitions

Contents

Chapter One

War and Power

*Today, the United States is the most powerful country in the world. It has the most **economic** power. It has the strongest army. It influences other countries' governments.*

But that wasn't always true. Other places have been more powerful. And they were around a lot longer. Think of the Roman Empire long ago. It ruled for hundreds of years. The United States is still pretty young. The country is only about 250 years old. There are lots of countries that are much older. And the United States didn't always have so much power.

So how did it happen? How did this young nation get so much power in such a short period of time?

It happened mostly because of a war. World War I helped launch the United States into such a powerful position.

World War I began in 1914. It lasted for more than four years. It was terrible. Many, many people died. Europe was filled with barbed-wire fences, land mines, trenches, and poison gas.

Many European cities and towns were badly damaged by the heavy fighting during World War I.

Almost **5 million** people served in the U.S. military during World War I.

About **320,000 American soldiers** lost their lives or were injured in the war.

The Western Front extended for more than **400 miles** (645 kilometers).

Two sides were fighting in the war. On one side were the Central Powers. They were Germany, Austria–Hungary, the Ottoman Empire, and Bulgaria. On the other side were the Allied forces. At the start of the war, the Allied countries included Great Britain, France, Belgium, and Russia.

Germany faced off against Great Britain and France on the Western Front. This was a line drawn down Europe. Lots of people died fighting on the Western Front. Some **civilians** got caught in between.

Until 1917, the United States was not involved with the war. Neither side was really winning or losing during the first three years. People were dying on both sides, but nothing was being accomplished. Then, the United States joined the Allies. That changed things.

The United States sent more and more soldiers to Europe. Pretty soon, the Allies were winning battles. And they were winning the war. In 1918, the German leader stepped down. Then, the Germans accepted a ceasefire. The war was over.

In 1918, the United States president was Woodrow Wilson. He announced the end of the war to the United States. Then, he started thinking about how to rebuild Europe. The war had destroyed a lot of things.

President Wilson didn't think that the winners should take revenge on the losers. They shouldn't still be angry about the war. Then, Europe would have peace. In Europe, though, many people were still angry. The Allies wanted to punish Germany. They wanted Germany to pay billions of dollars to make up for the war. Germans couldn't afford that. They had to rebuild their country.

After the United States entered World War I, the government created advertisements urging people to join the U.S. Army.

The Allies also wanted Germany to get rid of its weapons, so that it would not be able to attack other nations again. So, Germans destroyed their guns, trains, planes, and submarines. Germany had no more power, and it was poor.

Meanwhile, President Wilson wanted to start something called the League of Nations. The League of Nations would be an organization of all the countries of the world. He thought it would prevent a war from happening again. Countries could talk about their problems in the League instead of fight over them.

President Wilson traveled around the country by train, speaking to Americans about why he thought the League of Nations was important.

Americans didn't really like the League of Nations. They didn't want other countries having any say over the decisions the United States made. The United States didn't end up joining the League of Nations, even though it was the American president's idea. Congress had to approve the United States joining the league, and it refused to do so.

After World War I, the United States focused on its own affairs. Lots of things happened after the war. Not all of them were good.

During World War I, a group called the communists took over Russia. The communists believed that the government should own all property, like land. Everyone would work together to make life good for all. The United States is **capitalist**. Americans didn't like communists because they believed something different than capitalists.

Some people in the United States thought that communists might cause problems here. They wanted to crush any communist ideas. The government started spying on people it suspected might be communists. It sent some people to jail.

Vladimir Lenin started the Russian Communist Party. He led Russia from 1917 to 1924.

At the same time, the 1920s were called the Roaring Twenties. People were trying to have a good time after the war. Movies became popular. At first, they were silent—they didn't have sound. Then, filmmakers figured out how to add sound to the movies. Jazz music was also big. Jazz has African American roots, but in the Roaring Twenties, everyone was enjoying it. People could listen to jazz on the radio, another popular piece of entertainment.

Things we take for granted today were new in the 1920s. Electricity in homes was a big deal. Not many people had electricity at home before World War I. Afterward, many more homes were powered with electricity.

Cars became cheaper. Ordinary people could buy cars. That changed the way people got to work or took vacations, and it also changed what the landscape of the United States looked like.

People moved out of cities. Now that they could go places easily by car, they could live outside of the city. They moved to suburbs, which were brand new back then.

The United States was feeling pretty good about itself. It had proven it was a world power during World War I. And now many Americans were getting rich and enjoying themselves.

The Jazz Singer, made in 1927, was the first full-length movie to have a sound track that included dialogue, or talking. Earlier movies had only music or sound effects.

Three Decades of Firsts

In the three decades from 1900 to 1929, Americans produced many inventions and other advances that made life easier for most people and gave them more time to enjoy themselves.

1902

Willis Carrier makes the first air conditioner.

1907

The electric washing machine is invented. By 1928, nearly 1 million machines had been sold in the United States.

1908

The first plastic is invented. Called Bakelite, it is soon used to make parts for radios, automobiles, lamps, and other products.

1913

The modern factory assembly line begins to produce cars much faster and at lower cost than in the past.

1914

The Panama Canal opens, allowing ships to transport goods quickly between the U.S. East and West Coasts.

1920s

Electric refrigerators replace ice-cooled boxes. Food can be kept longer and more easily without spoiling.

Chapter Two

The Great Depression

The good times didn't last long. In 1929, the Great Depression hit America. This was a hard time in which many people were out of work and had little money. The Great Depression affected Americans of all sorts. It affected people all over the world.

At the beginning of the 1920s, the people who were having a good time in America wanted to buy all the popular new things. But they didn't always have the money to buy them. Instead, they used something called credit. People could buy something now. Then, they could pay for it later, either a little at a time or all at once. They were in debt until they paid.

Individual people did this. So did companies. To pay their debts, companies sold stock to people. Buying stock is like buying tiny shares of the ownership of a company.

People who bought stock in the early 1900s received papers called stock certificates, proving how many shares of a company they owned.

The New York Stock Exchange, on Wall Street in New York City, was the largest U.S. stock market in the 1920s. It still is today.

If a company does well, then the value of its stock goes up. Stockholders, or people who own that stock, make money. If a company does poorly, its stock value goes down. Stockholders lose money. A stock market is a place where the buying and selling of shares occurs. Investing money in the stock market became pretty popular in the 1920s. People were excited about getting rich by buying and selling stock.

But people didn't always have enough money to buy the stocks they wanted either. They used credit to buy stock

So now, lots of people and companies were in debt. No one had any money to pay for anything. But they kept on buying. Something had to give. First, houses got cheaper. People started buying less. But the stock market did better and better.

THE DUST BOWL

*Beginning in 1931, a severe **drought** in the Midwest and southern plains made the Great Depression even worse. Farmland turned to dust. Crops shriveled, animals died, and windstorms blew the soil away. The area affected was called the Dust Bowl.*

Many farm families had to move to the cities to find work. Others streamed west to California. They wanted to get to farms where they could work again. Eight years later, rain fell and the Dust Bowl was over.

Then, in 1929, the prices of stocks started falling. They kept falling. People panicked. They sold all their stocks. When they sold all their stocks, the value of the stocks dropped. It was a vicious circle. In the end, everything came crashing down.

Now, things were bad. People lost all their money. No one could afford to buy anything. Companies had to close down. They fired thousands of people. Americans without jobs couldn't pay for homes or for food. It was a hard life for lots of Americans.

The Great Depression lasted through all of the 1930s. It affected other countries too. The United States economy was tied to other countries' economies. If the United States did badly, so did other nations.

During the Great Depression, Americans weren't very happy with President Herbert Hoover. They thought he hadn't done enough to prevent the Great Depression. Franklin D. Roosevelt ran for president in 1932. He promised to help people, and he won the election.

President Roosevelt came up with a plan to help the country. It was called the New Deal. It put people back to work. Under the plan, Americans built lots of buildings, roads, and bridges paid for by the government. Congress made laws so that something like the Great Depression wouldn't happen again.

Some people liked the New Deal. It was helping the country. Some didn't. They thought it gave the president and the government too much power. They thought it made the American economic system less capitalist and a little more like communism.

Through it all, President Roosevelt held "fireside chats." He talked to Americans on the radio. He explained what was going on in the United States and what the government was doing.

In 1933, nearly **one-fourth** of all American workers had no jobs.

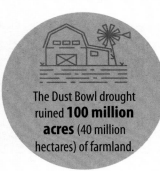
The Dust Bowl drought ruined **100 million acres** (40 million hectares) of farmland.

A New Deal program known as the WPA provided jobs for **8.5 million people**.

GET THINKING

Government Power

Often in U.S. history, Americans have disagreed about how much power the federal, or national, government should have. Some people think it is important for the government to run programs intended to help people in need or improve some aspect of American life. Others believe such programs can be too expensive and may limit people's freedom to do what they want without government rules. What do you think about the arguments for and against an active government that runs many programs?

Chapter Three
Another World War

For a while, there was no end in sight to the Great Depression. But then things changed. Unfortunately, what ended the Great Depression was another war.

People thought that World War I would be the last large conflict involving many nations. No one wanted a repeat. But it happened again. World War I had involved mostly Europe and North America, but World War II really was a world war. This time, people all over the world got involved.

Soup kitchens to feed the poor were common in Germany between World Wars I and II.

Just like in World War I, there were the Allied forces. Great Britain, France, the **Soviet Union**, the United States, and others were on the Allied side. On the other side were the Axis Powers. They included Germany, Italy, and Japan.

The war took a while to get started. While the United States was struggling through the Great Depression, things were happening in Germany as well. The country was still dealing with the effects of World War I. It didn't have much money. And other countries looked down on it.

Germans wanted someone to fix their country. They wanted to feel proud of their nation again. A man named Adolf Hitler promised to do the job. The people who supported him were called Nazis.

Hitler thought that the best Germans were those he called "Aryans." These were people with light skin, blonde or brown hair, and light-colored eyes. He thought these people were better than everyone else. Hitler blamed other people for Germany's problems. He blamed Jews. He blamed communists.

Soon, Hitler was very powerful. He controlled the whole government. But Hitler wanted to control more than just Germany. He wanted to take over Europe. First, he took over nearby countries. The rest of the world just let him. People didn't want another war.

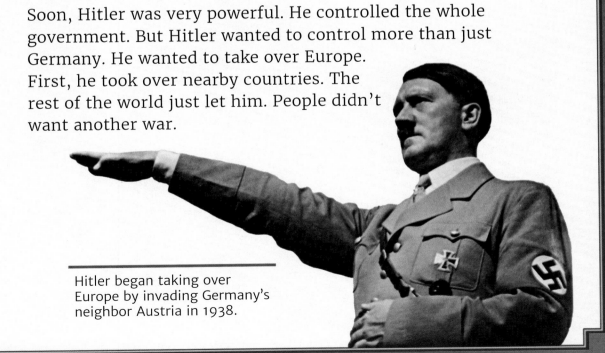

Hitler began taking over Europe by invading Germany's neighbor Austria in 1938.

More problems were going on in other parts of the world, too. In Asia, Japan was getting more powerful. Its army was getting bigger. It invaded China. The Japanese army killed people and bombed Chinese cities.

Germany invaded Poland next, in 1939. Finally, the world responded. Great Britain and France declared war on Germany. World War II began.

The Germans looked unstoppable. Hitler took over more and more countries. He even defeated France in less than a year. Now, it was mostly Britain all by itself against Germany. In June 1941, Germany invaded the Soviet Union, and that country joined the Allies.

So far, the United States didn't want to fight in the war. Americans wanted to stay out of what was going on in Europe and in Asia.

German troops quickly defeated Poland's armed forces. The German army held victory parades in Polish cities.

But they did take sides. Japan kept on taking over countries in Asia. The United States decided to stop selling oil and metal to Japan. Without oil and metal, Japan couldn't keep attacking other countries.

The Japanese were mad. They took action. On December 7, 1941, Japanese planes bombed Pearl Harbor in Hawai'i. The United States kept Navy warships and weapons there.

Japan also attacked United States forces in other parts of the Pacific Ocean. Americans couldn't ignore the war anymore. Now they were being attacked.

Hawai'i was almost the only part of the United States that the fighting ever actually reached. No one ever fought on the mainland. But that doesn't mean that the war didn't affect Americans.

Many ships were sunk or damaged during the bombing of Pearl Harbor, and more than 2,300 people serving in the U.S. military were killed.

World War II was the end of the Great Depression in the United States. Now, the United States needed people to make war goods. Workers flooded into factories to make guns and tanks and other things. People had jobs again.

The government controlled the prices of things. It **rationed** food and gasoline. The United States needed those things for the war. Americans couldn't use them all at home.

Now, there actually weren't enough workers anymore. Companies had to find new people to hire so that America's factories could make the things the war needed. Most men were in the army—so companies hired women.

Lots of women went to work in factories and other places. It was the first time that some women had even thought of working outside the home. This was a big change.

President Roosevelt kept being president. He was elected four times. That meant he led the United States longer than any other president in history. Now, presidents can be elected only two times at most.

During his fourth term, Roosevelt died. Vice President Harry S. Truman took over. Truman had to lead the country through the end of the war.

The U.S. government urged American women to help in the war effort. Women worked in factories that made weapons and built ships and planes.

THE AMERICAN CONCENTRATION CAMPS

Hitler put Jews and other people he didn't like in terrible places called concentration camps. Millions of people died there.

During World War II, the United States had its own concentration camps, called internment camps. After the bombing of Pearl Harbor, many Americans didn't trust Japanese people living in the United States. They thought these people might side with Japan and hurt the United States. There was no evidence for this idea. Really, it was just **racism**.

The government decided to round up thousands of Japanese Americans. They were sent by train to remote camps and forced to live there. These camps weren't as bad as the Nazi concentration camps. The point wasn't to kill everyone in them. It was just to keep them separate. But they were still horrible and cruel.

Some Italian Americans and German Americans were also put in camps since the United States was fighting Italy and Germany. Italians and Germans not in camps couldn't travel freely or carry cameras. War does terrible things!

The war went on for many years. In Europe, the Nazis were doing terrible things. Hitler wanted to get rid of all those people that he said had caused Germany's problems. He forced them into concentration camps where he killed millions of people.

The Nazis especially hated the Jews. They also killed other people they thought were not as good as Aryans or who believed in certain religions. Today, the term "Holocaust" is used to describe the Nazis' program of killing people. The term especially applies to the murders of Jewish people. The Nazis killed 6 million Jewish people by the end of World War II.

Slowly, the tide started turning against Germany. The Germans lost some major battles in the Soviet Union and elsewhere. Then, the Allies attacked German-controlled France. The attack was called D-Day. Many Allied troops landed on the coast of Normandy, in northwestern France. They fought with the Germans. Many people died. But the Allies won. They broke through the German army and freed France.

Small boats called landing craft brought Allied soldiers to five different beaches on D-Day. The troops faced heavy fire from German machine guns and artillery when they landed.

Eventually, the Allies captured Berlin, the capital of Germany. And then, Germany surrendered in May of 1945.

But there was still the war in Asia. The United States was winning, but Japan kept fighting. People thought the war might drag on forever.

More than **100 million soldiers** fought in World War II.

But it wouldn't. The United States was creating a new weapon. It was the atomic bomb. President Truman had to decide whether to use it or not. It was far more powerful than any other weapon created up to that time. Truman gave the Japanese a warning. They didn't listen.

The **U.S. Army** grew from 268,000 soldiers in 1940 to **8.3 million** in 1945.

On August 6, 1945, the United States dropped an atomic bomb on the city of Hiroshima. Eighty thousand Japanese died instantly. More died later from **radiation** poisoning. Still Japan didn't give up. On August 9, the United States dropped another atomic bomb on Nagasaki. It killed even more people. Finally, Japan surrendered.

About **64 million** people, including millions of civilians, died during World War II.

GET THINKING

To Bomb or Not?

People have questioned President Truman's decision to use weapons as destructive as the atomic bombs. In total, more than 260,000 people lost their lives as a result of the August 1945 bombings. But if Japan continued to fight much longer, hundreds of thousands more American and Japanese soldiers could have been killed. Such powerful bombs, Truman thought, would scare the Japanese into surrendering. What do you think about Truman's decision? Was it the right thing to do? Why or why not?

World War II Battles in Europe

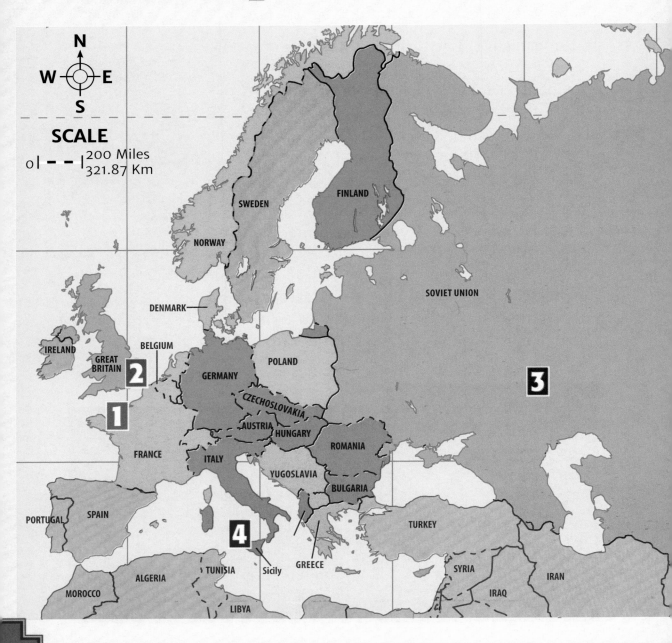

N W E S

SCALE
0 |– – –| 200 Miles
321.87 Km

NORWAY
SWEDEN
FINLAND
SOVIET UNION
DENMARK
IRELAND
GREAT BRITAIN
BELGIUM
2
1
GERMANY
POLAND
3
CZECHOSLOVAKIA
AUSTRIA
HUNGARY
FRANCE
ITALY
ROMANIA
YUGOSLAVIA
BULGARIA
PORTUGAL
SPAIN
4
TURKEY
TUNISIA
Sicily
GREECE
SYRIA
IRAN
MOROCCO
ALGERIA
IRAQ
LIBYA

1 D-Day

D-Day was June 6, 1944. About 156,000 U.S., Canadian, and British soldiers landed on Normandy beaches. Today, a monument stands on Omaha Beach, where American troops fought.

2 Bombing of London

From September 1940 to May 1941, German planes bombed London and other areas of Great Britain. Hitler hoped to break the spirit of the British people, but he failed.

From July 1942 to February 1943, hundreds of thousands of German and Soviet soldiers fought near the Russian city of Stalingrad, now called Volgograd. The Soviet troops finally won. A statue in Volgograd honors its defenders.

3 Battle of Stalingrad

4 Sicily Invasion

The first place in Europe where U.S. soldiers fought was the Italian island of Sicily. U.S., British, and other Allied troops landed on Sicily in July 1943. By August, they had captured the island from Italian and German forces.

LEGEND

- ☐ Water
- ☐ Allied Powers
- ☐ Axis Powers
- ☐ Other Nations
- ☐ Axis-held

Chapter Four

Fighting Superpowers

For a very long time, Western Europe had the most power of any area on Earth. Countries such as France and Great Britain controlled much of the rest of the world. Now, it was different.

World War II had destroyed many Western European countries. They had to start over. Two other countries took over as the most powerful. Those were the United States and the Soviet Union. During World War II, the two countries had been Allies. But they didn't really get along. The Soviet Union was communist. And most Americans didn't like communists.

By the end of the war, Soviet forces had advanced across Eastern Europe and the eastern part of Germany. After the war, the Soviet Union kept control of these areas. It set up communist governments in East Germany and several Eastern European nations. It left Soviet soldiers in those countries.

Soviet soldiers stayed in East Germany for decades after World War II ended.

Many people in the United States thought the Soviet Union would try to further extend its power in Europe. President Truman came up with the Truman Doctrine. This policy said that the United States would basically help any country that was fighting communism. America would give these countries money and weapons. The United States ended up helping Greece and Turkey.

The United States also came up with the Marshall Plan. George Marshall was President Truman's secretary of state. He developed most of the plan.

The Marshall Plan gave money, equipment, and other aid to countries in Western Europe to help them rebuild. In Great Britain, France, and other nations, homes and factories were gone. People were sick or dead. Farms were destroyed. The United States sent food. It sent tractors so farmers could grow crops again.

THE BIRTH OF THE UNITED NATIONS

When the League of Nations failed to stop World War II, it ceased to exist. But the world needed another organization like it. The United Nations (UN) officially was born on October 24, 1945. China, France, the Soviet Union, Great Britain, and the United States, along with other member states, signed the agreement. The UN, which has its headquarters in New York City, still exists today.

The United States and the Soviet Union soon entered another war. But there wasn't really any direct fighting in this war. Armies didn't face off against each other. Guns weren't fired, and bombs weren't dropped.

Both countries wanted to be the only powerful nation. They didn't want the other one to have so much power.

Each tried to build nuclear weapons. These were more-advanced versions of the atomic bombs used against Japan. The United States had the first ones. But the Soviets weren't far behind. Soon, both countries had a large supply of very dangerous weapons.

Some U.S. nuclear bombs were put on missiles that could reach the Soviet Union. To protect the missiles, they were kept in underground concrete buildings called silos.

People were afraid of nuclear war. If anything happened, one country could bomb the other. Then, that one would fight back with its own bombs. The world would be destroyed in the process. No one could win.

Meanwhile, in China, there was a civil war. A civil war is when two parts of the same country fight against each other. Communist forces took over in 1949. China was now communist. So was nearby North Korea. The United States was worried that even more countries would become communist.

In 1950, North Korea invaded South Korea. South Korea wasn't communist. The United States wanted to keep it that way. The United States sent troops to stop the communists. China sent its army to fight for the North Koreans.

Neither side really won the Korean War. Armies fought for three years, but nothing changed. A lot of people died, though.

Communists had also taken over part of Vietnam, another country in Asia. A man named Ho Chi Minh was the leader there. He was a communist.

In 1954, the country was split into South Vietnam and communist North Vietnam. The United States supported South Vietnam. The U.S. government sent weapons and some soldiers to help make South Vietnam's army strong.

About 1.8 million U.S. troops took part in the Korean War. Today, the United States still keeps soldiers and tanks in South Korea to help protect it.

Many people in Vietnam wanted it to be one country. Some people agreed with Ho Chi Minh. They thought South Vietnam should become communist, too. A communist group in the south called the Vietcong fought for Vietnam to become one country.

North Vietnam sent soldiers south to help the Vietcong. The United States sent more and more soldiers to South Vietnam to fight against the communist forces. The Vietnam War lasted for a very long time. In 1968, the North Vietnamese started winning.

THE McCARTHY ERA

One senator really wanted to get rid of communism in the United States. That was Senator Joseph McCarthy. He got government employees fired if they were suspected of liking communism. He accused people of being communists even when he had no evidence. His fear affected the whole country. Libraries threw out books with ties to communism. Actors, artists, professors, and others couldn't find jobs if they agreed with communism or were suspected of agreeing with it. Some high schools even required students to sign loyalty oaths to the U.S. government before they could receive their diplomas. By 1954, the country was tired of McCarthy. The public turned against him and his hunt for communists.

Back in the United States, people were angry. They wanted the war to end. There were huge protests. Finally, all U.S. troops left Vietnam in 1973. Two years later, North Vietnam took over South Vietnam.

During the 1960s, the United States was also worried about another country. A communist named Fidel Castro had taken over Cuba. This island lies to the south of the eastern United States.

John F. Kennedy became the U.S. president in 1961. That year, the United States helped a small force invade Cuba. The force landed at the Bay of Pigs. The attack was a complete disaster. Castro's soldiers easily defeated the invaders.

In November 1969, more than 500,000 people demonstrated in Washington, D.C., against the Vietnam War.

During the Cuban Missile Crisis, U.S. planes closely watched Soviet ships carrying missiles.

The Soviet Union was helping Cuba. In 1962, the Soviets started building missile bases there. Bomb-carrying missiles shot from Cuba would reach the United States very quickly. The U.S. government demanded that the Soviets remove the missile bases.

For a while, the world held its breath. Everyone knew there could be a nuclear war. This tense time is known as the Cuban Missile Crisis. Then, President Kennedy talked to the Soviets. The United States and the Soviet Union agreed to a compromise. Nobody would use any nuclear weapons.

There were several American presidents during the Cold War. After Harry Truman left the White House, President Dwight Eisenhower took over. He had been a general during World War II.

After Eisenhower came John F. Kennedy. He was also called JFK. He was a very popular president. He wanted Americans to think positively and to do great things. He also helped create the space program that sent Americans into space.

Millions were shocked when a gunman killed JFK in 1963. Vice President Lyndon Johnson took over. Johnson was elected president for one term after that.

Then came Richard Nixon. People had many strong opinions both for and against Nixon. He promised to end the Vietnam War, so he got elected in 1968. He didn't end it until several years later, though.

Nixon ended up resigning as president. During and after his 1972 reelection campaign, Nixon and people who worked for him did some illegal things. He was afraid he wouldn't be reelected. He had people break into his opponents' headquarters in a group of Washington, D.C., buildings called the Watergate.

Nixon got in a lot of trouble for that. It was called the Watergate scandal. Before he could be fired, he resigned. His vice president, Gerald Ford, became president then. Jimmy Carter was the next president, after Ford.

Besides wars, other things were going on during this time. Lots of changes happened after World War II. Young people especially did things differently. They listened to different music. They had different ideas about how people should live their lives. They wore different clothes. They let their hair grow long, and many young men grew beards.

The U.S. space program started by President Kennedy succeeded, in 1969, in sending the first people to land on the Moon.

The Civil Rights Movement also happened during this time. A lot of people spoke out to try to make sure African Americans were treated equally. African Americans had faced hatred and many types of **discrimination**. Some states tried to keep African Americans from voting. In a number of areas, African-American children had to go to separate schools, which were often not as good as the schools white children attended. Sometimes, African Americans could not go to the same restaurants as whites or even sit in the same section of a bus or train as white people.

Martin Luther King, Jr., was the most famous civil rights leader. He urged all people to struggle for African Americans' rights. King also said the struggle should be peaceful. He was against using violence to try to gain equal rights for African Americans.

At a 1963 demonstration called the March on Washington for Jobs and Freedom, Martin Luther King, Jr., spoke to the crowd about his dream for equality for all Americans.

King won the Nobel Peace Prize for his work. But not everyone agreed with King. Some people who were racist hated him. They didn't like that he was changing America. One of his enemies shot and killed him in 1968.

Women also faced various kinds of discrimination. For example, they were unable to get hired for many types of jobs. When women did work, they often received lower pay than men doing the same or very similar work. Many people took part in the Women's Movement to gain greater rights for women.

Lots of things were going on in the 1950s, 1960s, and 1970s. Some of these were good things. Some of them were terrible things. Through it all, the United States started looking a lot more like it does today.

There were **separate schools** for African Americans in **21 states** when the U.S. Supreme Court outlawed such schools in 1954.

Congress passed the **Voting Rights Act**, in **1965**, to try to make sure African Americans were allowed to vote.

In 1965, the average salary of **women** workers was **60 percent** of what men earned on average.

GET THINKING

Does Might Make Right?

After World War II, many European powers gave up their colonies. Some of the new independent countries in Africa considered becoming communist. In Angola, a civil war started. The Soviet Union backed the communists with money and weapons. The United States provided weapons and aid to the other side. The Soviet Union and United States each thought it was helping the right side. Is it right for stronger nations to interfere in another country's government, even if they think it is for that country's own good? What do you think, and why?

Chapter Five
Last Superpower Standing

By the 1980s, the Cold War was ending. The Soviet Union started getting weaker. But the United States stayed strong.

The Soviet government made a lot of mistakes. It scared people and treated them badly. It took over other countries that didn't want to be under its control.

In 1985, Mikhail Gorbachev became the leader of the Soviet Union. He decided that communism wasn't really working. Gorbachev wanted to make the Soviet Union's economy grow. He made some changes. He worked with U.S. President Ronald Reagan. So much happened that communism came crashing down.

Beginning in 1989, the Soviet Union lost control of East Germany and countries in Eastern Europe. This gave many areas their freedom. In 1991, the Soviet Union itself broke up into Russia and 14 other countries.

All of a sudden, the Cold War was over. The United States was the only superpower left. There was no other strong country to rival it.

In the late 1980s, large protests were held in several Eastern European countries, such as Czechoslovakia, demanding an end to Soviet control.

THE BERLIN WALL

The Berlin Wall was built by the East German government in 1961 to cut in half the German city of Berlin. East Berlin was part of East Germany. West Berlin was part of West Germany, a country created after World War II with the help of the United States, Great Britain, and France.

West Germany did a lot better after the war. East Germany got poorer. Many East Germans escaped to West Germany. The Berlin Wall was supposed to stop that. The wall kept families and friends apart. Almost no one could cross.

Germans hated the wall. Eventually, the East German government became too weak to continue. In 1989, wall guards started tearing down the wall. Lots of regular people helped too. The Soviet Union couldn't do anything to stop them. Tearing down the Berlin Wall symbolized the end of the Cold War. By 1990, East Germany had joined with West Germany.

The United States sent almost 700,000 troops to the Middle East for the Persian Gulf War.

With all the power that the United States had at the end of the Cold War came choices about how to use it. Some people have not been happy with how the United States has used its power.

There were more wars following the Cold War. The first one was the Persian Gulf War, after Iraq invaded Kuwait. The United States went to war to defend Kuwait, a country in the Middle East. It was a short war. It only lasted about seven months. The United States won, but a lot of Iraqi people died.

Meanwhile, at home in America, the economy was in trouble. In the 1980s, things were hard for a lot of people. The number of people without jobs increased. Some people thought the government was spending too much money. It wasn't as bad as the Great Depression, though.

Bill Clinton and George H. W. Bush held several debates, shown on television, during the 1992 presidential campaign. Many viewers thought Clinton better understood average people's problems. This helped him win the election.

President George H. W. Bush tried to fix things. He wasn't very successful. In 1992, Americans voted Bill Clinton into office instead. The 1990s ended up being very prosperous. Now people had jobs, and they were making money. The economy was healthier.

President Clinton was very popular for most of his time as president. However, he did get into trouble during his last couple years.

People found out that Clinton had been too close to an intern in the White House. Then he had lied about it.

The government investigated. In Congress, the House of Representatives decided to **impeach** him. Clinton was not convicted of doing anything wrong. He finished up his term as president.

Then, there was a presidential election in 2000. Clinton's vice president, Al Gore, ran against George W. Bush. Bush was the son of the former President George H. W. Bush.

The election was very close. There was a dispute about counting votes in Florida. The Supreme Court settled the dispute, and Bush ended up becoming president. Not everyone was happy, though. Bush's election divided many Americans.

Life in America changed hugely on September 11, 2001. That day, a plane flew into a tower of the World Trade Center in New York City. People couldn't believe it. They didn't know what had happened. They thought it was an accident.

The September 11, 2001, terrorist actions against the World Trade Center and other targets were the deadliest attack on the United States in the country's history.

Then, a second plane crashed into the other tower. This clearly wasn't an accident. Pretty soon, Americans found out that terrorists had hijacked four planes. One flew into the Pentagon near Washington, D.C. The other crashed in a field in Pennsylvania.

September 11 shocked the world. Thousands of people died. The United States was not as safe as people had thought.

Osama bin Laden often spoke against the United States in radio and television messages.

The government soon figured out who was responsible. It was a group called al Qaeda. Al Qaeda was an extreme Islamic group. A man named Osama bin Laden was in charge of it. This group didn't like the United States getting involved in the Middle East.

Bin Laden was hiding in Afghanistan. But Afghanistan refused to hand him over to the United States. A group called the Taliban ruled the country.

The United States sent soldiers to Afghanistan. The goal was to get rid of the Taliban and to kill bin Laden. This was the start of the "War on Terror." Two months later, the Taliban was beaten back, though not totally defeated. Bin Laden was still on the loose.

VOTE

Al Gore received about **544,000 more votes** than George W. Bush in the 2000 election.

Nearly **3,000 people** died in the attacks on September 11, 2001.

U.S. troops finally found and killed **Osama bin Laden** on **May 2, 2011**.

The United States was already involved with one war in Afghanistan. Then, it started another one in Iraq.

President Bush decided that Iraq must have dangerous weapons. He called them "weapons of mass destruction." Bush was afraid that Iraq would use them against the United States. In 2003, he sent in the military to find the weapons.

U.S. troops captured Baghdad, the capital of Iraq. Saddam Hussein, the **dictator** who ruled Iraq, fled. He was captured a few months later, though. No one found any weapons of mass destruction.

Colin Powell, President Bush's secretary of state, told the United Nations that the United States had evidence Iraq was holding weapons of mass destruction.

President Bush declared that the United States had won the war in Iraq. But fighting didn't end. It lasted for a long time. Many people in Iraq didn't like Americans being there. They formed groups to fight the American soldiers. Some of these groups also fought against each other. Many people died on all sides.

Around the end of the 20th century, there were good things and bad things going on in the United States. Many Americans were focusing on the two wars being fought. But the economy was doing well. People were living their lives. And the United States was still the strongest country in the world.

In 2003, President Bush gave a speech stating that the U.S. military could consider its "mission accomplished" in Iraq. Later, Bush was criticized for this speech, since U.S. troops continued fighting in Iraq for eight more years.

Timeline

1914—World War I begins in Europe.

1931—A severe drought starts in the Midwest, causing the Dust Bowl.

1939—Germany invades Poland, and World War II begins.

1910	1920	1930	1940

1932—Franklin D. Roosevelt is elected president.

1929—The stock market crashes, and the Great Depression begins.

1962—President John F. Kennedy leads the nation through the Cuban Missile Crisis.

2001—Terrorists attack the United States on September 11.

| 1945 | 1965 | 1985 | 2005 |

1945—In a ceremony on a U.S. warship, Japan agrees to stop fighting, ending World War II.

1989—As the Cold War nears an end, the Berlin Wall is torn down.

1968—Civil rights leader Martin Luther King, Jr., is killed.

Quiz

ONE
In what year was the Union Nations officially established?

TWO
What is the term for two parts of the same country fighting each other?

THREE
On what date did two planes fly into the World Trade Center towers?

FOUR
Where in Cuba did a small invasion force helped by the United States land in 1961?

FIVE
What is the name of the scandal that led President Richard Nixon to resign?

SIX
Who became president of the United States after Harry Truman?

SEVEN
Who was the leader of Germany during World War II?

EIGHT
Where did Japanese planes attack the United States on December 7, 1941?

NINE
What were the 1920s called, because people were having a good time?

TEN
Who was the leader of al Qaeda in 2001?

Key Words

capitalist: describes an economic system in which land, factories, and other property are owned and controlled by individuals, not the government

civilians: people who are not in the military

dictator: a ruler who has all the power in a country or area

discrimination: unfair treatment based on people's race, cultural group, gender, or religion

drought: a long period of time with little or no rain

economic: relating to a nation's money, land, workers, and natural resources and the way it uses those resources to produce goods and services

impeach: to charge a public official with improper behavior while in office

racism: hatred toward and unfair treatment of a group of people based on the group's race

radiation: a powerful and dangerous form of energy. Atomic bomb explosions release large amounts of radiation.

rationed: controlled the amount of something that people can use

Soviet Union: a nation formed in 1922 that included Russia and surrounding areas

Index

LIGHTB⬡X

⊕ SUPPLEMENTARY RESOURCES

Click on the plus icon ⊕ found in the bottom left corner of each spread to open additional teacher resources.

- Download and print the book's quizzes and activities
- Access curriculum correlations
- Explore additional web applications that enhance the Lightbox experience

LIGHTBOX DIGITAL TITLES
Packed full of integrated media

VIDEOS
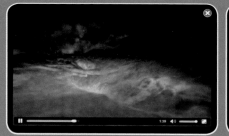

INTERACTIVE MAPS
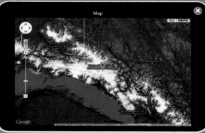

WEBLINKS

SLIDESHOWS

QUIZZES

OPTIMIZED FOR
- ✓ **TABLETS**
- ✓ **WHITEBOARDS**
- ✓ **COMPUTERS**
- ✓ **AND MUCH MORE!**

Published by Smartbook Media Inc.
350 5th Avenue, 59th Floor
New York, NY 10118
Website: www.openlightbox.com

Published by Mason Crest in 2013

062018
121117

Library of Congress Cataloging-in-Publication Data
Names: South, Victor, author.
Title: America in the 20th century (1913/1999) / Victor South.
Description: New York, NY : Smartbook Media Inc., [2019] | Series: How America became America | Includes index. | Audience: Grades 4-6. | Identifiers: LCCN 2017054972 (print) | LCCN 2018005553 (ebook) | ISBN 9781510536111 (Multi User ebook) | ISBN 9781510536104 (hardcover : alk. paper)
Subjects: LCSH: United States--History--20th century--Juvenile literature. | United States--History, Military--20th century--Juvenile literature. | United States--Foreign relations--20th century--Juvenile literature.
Classification: LCC E741 (ebook) | LCC E741 .S66 2019 (print) | DDC 973.9--dc23
LC record available at https://lccn.loc.gov/2017054972

Printed in Brainerd, Minnesota, United States
1 2 3 4 5 6 7 8 9 0 22 21 20 19 18

Project Coordinator Heather Kissock
Art Director Terry Paulhus

Photo Credits
Every reasonable effort has been made to trace ownership and to obtain permission to reprint copyright material. The publisher would be pleased to have any errors or omissions brought to its attention so that they may be corrected in subsequent printings.

The publisher acknowledges Getty Images, Alamy, and iStock as its primary image suppliers for this title.